THE PEACE
WITHIN

THE PEACE
WITHIN

P. A. WILSON

Library of Congress Control Number: 2009913639
ISBN: Hardcover   978-1-4500-1530-1
               Softcover   978-1-4500-1529-5
               Ebook   978-1-4500-1531-8

This book was printed in the United States of America.

To order additional copies of this book, contact:
Xlibris Corporation
1-888-795-4274
www.Xlibris.com
Orders@Xlibris.com
70715

Contents

Chapter 1   What a Day! 11

Chapter 2   Almost Daybreak 19

Chapter 3   An Awakening 23

Chapter 4   Revelation I 27

Chapter 5   Revelation II...41

Chapter 6   A Lesson Learned...51

Chapter 7   Who Really Knows?.......................................67

This book is dedicated to my husband, William Wilson, who passed way on February 10, 1991, who constantly encouraged me to write and to fulfill my lifelong dream.

A special thank you to our loving daughters, Cynthia and Lori; granddaughters, Shawntrice and Jertasia; son-in-law, Shawn, and countless friends and family for their prayers, constant support, and for being a perfect captive audience through continuous revelations, numerous updates, and jubilant responses. In addition, a special acknowledgement to my parents, Mrs. Irma Burton and the late Mr. J. C. Burton, for their love, support, and for being outstanding role models.

After all of these truly blessed people, I was given a dynamic publishing company, Xlibris, and I would like to thank them for making every step a truly remarkable one. Finally, most of all, giving honor to God for His guiding hand and for the peace that I experienced throughout the total writing process.

Thank you all!

"I can do all things through Christ who strengthens me."
Philippians 4:13

Special thanks to Lori Wilson for taking the author photo and Mrs. Janice Hodge for helping the author in capturing images for the front cover and the interior part of the book.

Chapter 1

What a Day!

The silent stillness and the gentle October breeze, coupled with the miraculous colors of the season painted a picture that was imprinted in my memory. As I look back, the picturesque scene of that day resembled those of an orange as it changed from lime green to lemon yellow to golden orange. The day was as peaceful as the calm before the storm and as beautiful as a new blossoming butterfly. The crisp autumn air lingered with a hint of expectation. Buried in the distance by the rising clouds was the golden glare of the sun. The pumpkin-colored leaves of the trees danced about on the ground. All seemed peaceful until the stillness and admiration of the evening was broken by a soft knock at the door. My mother swiftly moved to the door, and peering from the other side was my Aunt Aimee. She quickly and quietly entered with a mouselike appearance. She was clothed in a full-length smoky gray-colored sweater coat with a hood that hid her face and her outfit. It was as strange as wearing costumes to a family gathering or arriving at a wedding after the bride had thrown the bouquet. A silent movie couldn't have had a more dramatic effect.

My Aunt Aimee had always been a frequent visitor, but this time was different. This time everyone acted as though they had a part to play. Everyone was so hush-hush as though they were waiting for something to happen. There was my mother that had a look that implied, "Just don't ask." Then there was my father that completely stayed out of the way and tended to his regular routine, but with a look that screamed, *"I can't believe this!"* Then there were my sisters and my brothers that were completely dumbfounded like they had walked into the movie theater and had watched the end just before the credits realizing that they were too early for the scheduled movie, but too late for the one ending. You know that look. Since the end is known, should I stay or should I leave? Lastly, there I was—who had sensed that something was a bit unsettling, but since I was always told that I was her favorite niece, I wondered if I should just remain silent. So I just stood there actually gripping my lips with my teeth to keep the words from escaping and tried to keep the look off my face. I believe that it worked. Still, we just stood there like robots all playing the same game, "Don't Look Too Closely," for what seemed like more than an hour, but in actuality, it was only a few moments.

I am getting ahead of myself. Let me recount to the best of my recollection what happened on that eerie fall day in 1972. My name is Ino, and at the age of about eleven, my Aunt Aimee came to visit us from a small town in Alabama. It was supposed to be a very short visit, but it turned into an extended stay. It wasn't that she didn't have a home, she did, but something we were told had happened that sent her to live with us for a while. *Why us?* We didn't have a large house, but we did have a large family. We lived in Alabama also, but in a quiet neighborhood where people were friendly, caring, family oriented, depended on each other, knew just enough about one another to stay out of each other's business. This was a community where people were considerate and compassionate, helping hand kind of people like Mr. and Mrs. Thompson or like Ms. Elsie Watkins or Miss Lula Mae. This was our neighborhood, and my Aunt Aimee fit in perfectly. To be honest, I don't think anyone outside the immediate family realized that she was there at all. It was as though she was planted in the right neighborhood at the right time. It was like a made-for-television presentation, but we were living it.

As I look back, her visit, to say the least, was an eye-opening experience for my entire family. Like I said before, my aunt visited frequently, but we really didn't *know* her until this uncanny visit. I'm sure that you understand about not really knowing someone until you see them in a different light, and that's the way it was with my Aunt Aimee. Take this one time, the night that she moved in, did I say moved in, I meant, came for a visit. When she arrived, we all looked at one another in amazement with this look, "Where is she going to sleep? We have only three bedrooms, so who is going to lose their room?" You could see the puzzled looks on our faces as though we were saying, *"Who is it going to be?"* Little did I know that it was going to be *me.* Yes, that is correct. My parents or should I say my mother gave me the look, and I *just* knew. As I looked around, my entire family had it, but I had the look of "Who me?" I was truly hoping that this was a figment of my imagination, but I quickly realized that it was real when my mother asked me, "Would it be okay for Aimee to bunk with you?" *"Who me?"* My look conveyed. Then I quickly imprisoned the millions of thoughts that popped into my head so as not to have them plastered across my face. When I finally managed to lift my head, I looked into the gazing eyes of my entire family, and at that very moment, I realized that a speedy misalignment of my thoughts and emotions was in order, because I was about to be read like an old-time silent movie, and my family were the viewers.

Now I was an eleven-year-old child, a boarder myself because I was too young to pay the rent, so how was I supposed to respond to that question, "Well, I don't think so because I am paying for this room on a weekly basis."

Wake up! I was a child so all I could say was, "Come on in. I will help you get settled in my, ooohh excuse me, our room," and that's exactly what I did. My entire family couldn't believe the words that came out of my mouth because they did not match the thoughts plastered across my face. Well, I guess the alignment was off. Sometimes we do or say what is right, not necessarily what we want to do, and that's exactly what I did that day.

As I turned to walk into the bedroom, I realized that my family knew that really wasn't what I was thinking, so I avoided any eye contact. I will never forget the astonished looks embedded on their faces and the mimelike one painted on mine, as we entered the room, like I was never going to emerge the same. Still, with gaping mouths and wandering eyes, they watched me like I was committing a crime, but what else could I do? There was nothing that I could do. So

I placed her bags down and turned around with that phony look plastered across my face hoping that she would not see that I knew something was wrong.

And to my surprise, it worked and she said with a sly upward grin and a light pat on my left shoulder, "We are going to be roommates." Continuous thoughts flooded my mind like a river, but imprisonment at this point was impossible. They were out and running . . . *And where are you going to sleep? How long is this going to last?* This went on and on. Then I smiled hoping that my thoughts would not become apparent, but at this point, who could tell?

At that very moment, a steady beat of feet moved away from the door like a marching army, and about five minutes later, my mother entered. Again, many uncontrollable thoughts surfaced: *What took you so long? What are we supposed to do? Are we supposed to sleep in shifts, or one on the bed and the other on the floor? No disrespect intended.* I guess my mother read my face because she jumped in quicker than a young child discovering a sprinkler on a hot June afternoon.

"I'll make you a pallet on the floor," my mother said in a low calming voice, which implied for me to be patient since this was supposed to be a short visit. So I harnessed my thoughts, nodded and smiled simultaneously, and gave my mother a bear hug as an affirmation of our little secret. Then, almost inaudibly, I whispered a low good night, and in my tiredness fell awkwardly on the pallet that my mother had made for me and tried to doze off to sleep. While dozing I found it difficult to keep my eyes closed because I could not only see, but hear my mother and my aunt whispering as my aunt closed the door. What were they saying? As I drifted in and out of sleep, I watched snapshots of the day play across the mirrors to my soul. *What a day!*

Chapter 2

Almost Daybreak

After a day that I was longing to forget and a night of unending adventures, I was awakened by my aunt who was talking in her sleep. What was she saying? Should I listen or try to dismiss it? What if I heard something incriminating, what would I do with the information? Regardless, listening was not an option because this was /is my room. Who was George? Was this what she and my mother were talking about before she left the room? Should I continue to listen, take mental notes, tell my mother in the morning, or did my mother know already? What was she talking about and who was she talking to? With a rag doll appearance, I lay there limp and motionless but intently and expectantly listening for about twenty minutes. Interesting! If she did this tonight, I can't wait for tomorrow night. The thoughts just wouldn't stop and neither would the action that night. I wonder if she knows that she talks in her sleep. Should I tell her in the morning? What's that noise? The bed is squeaking! The door is opening! Should I look? Oh, no! Where is she going? Does she walk in her sleep, too? This is too much! Should I stop her, or will she remember anything in the morning? Should I . . . What's that? Back in position. Someone is bringing her back. Is it my mother? Does she know that her sister is a sleepwalker? On this floor, I can't see anyone, but a lavender scent just floated by and mixed with the vanilla scent that my Aunt Aimee always wore. Who else could it be? Still, who could be sure? What's the connection? The big question is, if my mother knew, then why am I in here? What if my aunt committed a crime while she was sleepwalking? Maybe that's what those looks were trying to tell me before I came in here. Were they saying, "Run!" But where? Run in or run out? Perish that thought, but after everything that has happened tonight, could it be possible? This was another made-for-television presentation and no retakes needed. I need to dismiss that thought and try to get some sleep. Well, I can hear my Aunt Aimee snoring again, so I think I'll try to get some sleep. Time will tell and it did. It seemed like it just happened yesterday.

Chapter 3

An Awakening

As daybreak crept through the shutters and danced on the pillows, the walls, and on me, I noticed that the door was slightly ajar, and there were sounds of the family waking up to a new day and unexpected adventures. Oh, what a night! Was it a dream, or was it real? I slowly looked around the room joyfully hoping, but quickly realizing that as much as I wanted it to be a dream to be continued another night, it was real. Listlessly stretched across my bed was all the proof that I needed, my Aunt Aimee. Since my bedroom opened into the kitchen, the night crew was there just as they had been when they watched me disappear from the peaceful life that I had known before. *Would things ever be the same again?* I thought.

Looking back now, for just a brief moment that morning, it was as though my Aunt Aimee was just visiting again, or maybe that's the way that I wanted it to be. That day turned into weeks then into months. My aunt stayed with us for six long months, and I slept on that floor night after night after night. I guess I should have realized that it was going to be a longer stay when my pallet changed into a twin-size mattress, but I was a child. Then one day I noticed her bags packed behind our bedroom door. It's easier to say our now since it's been so long. Then the next morning she gave us hugs and kisses, said thank-you and good-bye, and as quickly as she had appeared, she disappeared.

The next few days we were as busy as bees putting the house back in order. My mother aired out the room, cleaned, changed the sheets, and the room was mine again. I was no longer on the floor anymore. I was free to be myself again. Life was good! I could sleep in my own comfortable bed, and it didn't matter that I had to share my room with two of my sisters. Also, that feeling that had been with me for so long was gone, and it was replaced with the feeling of anticipation and longing that you get during the Christmas season. That's the feeling that I had that day! I had waited for that day for so long, and it had finally arrived. It was finally the way it used to be! Sometimes you don't appreciate what you have until you lose it. I had always heard this, but who would have thought that it could refer to *the peace within* me and my family. My younger sisters and brothers were laughing again, and the uneasy feeling that had been with me for months was gone. I felt a connection to my family again, an inner peace, and it felt good, extremely good.

Looking back, I realized that my Aunt Aimee needed that time to gain her inner peace, and by being around our family, she had the opportunity to experience a nurturing family environment and without responsibilities. She needed to be plugged into our family where she did not have to make decisions, where she did not have to worry about anything, and where she could get back to being herself. She needed to be a part of a home so that she could make her house a home.

Still, I missed my Aunt Aimee and her unique way of doing things. I missed seeing her food on the white metal cabinet in the kitchen with the invisible line separating hers from ours, choice this and that. I missed her vanilla-scented towels in the bathroom. I missed her countless cans of Vienna sausage lining the cabinet and jars and jars of creamy peanut butter and rows of crackers everywhere. All gone, all gone and so was my Aunt Aimee. I had gotten used to seeing her, and suddenly she had disappeared just the way she had appeared.

So while I rest on the milky white weatherworn porch swing on this beautiful Indian summer day, I couldn't help but reflect on that puzzling, yet eerie period in my life. The similarity of times past with the pumpkin-colored leaves dancing about on the ground as they danced so many years ago stirred memories, aroused creativity, and opened a door to the past. Still, remembering that quiet house with hushed walls and the unmentioned secret of my Aunt Aimee stirred both jubilant and somber emotions. To this day, I never told my mother anything about that night. My mother said that my aunt and her family moved far away and that she was a more compassionate person since that visit.

I know that my aunt benefited from her visit with us, but we also benefited. I realized that people aren't always what they seem, that you can always depend on your family, that all families have their secrets and ours is no exception, and that having inner peace is extremely satisfying. My aunt has moved on, but what was it all about? My name is Ino. My parents named me that from birth. It is short for *I know*.

Chapter 4

Revelation I

I received two letters today one from my mother and another from my sister Jamie. I was delighted to hear from both of them, especially my sister since I hadn't heard from her in about eight years. Even though I was excited to hear from my sister, I thought that I would read mother's letter first.

As I unfolded the pages of my mother's letter, a hint of lavender surfaced from the pink-flowered stationery and brushed my nostrils. Immediately, I had a flashback to that period when my Aunt Aimee was brought back into the room after sleepwalking. Each time there was a lavender scent that was mixed with the vanilla that my aunt always wore. Was it possible? Well, what do you know, it was my mother that brought her back. After all this time, my mother really did know. She stated that she wanted to tell me something but not over the telephone.

Her letter read,

Fall 1994

Dear Ino,

I hope that this letter finds you and Liam in good health. Yesterday I heard from your sister, and she told us that graduation day is on the nineteenth. She was so excited! I immediately wrote her back and informed her that since your father has been under the weather, we would not be able to attend, but maybe you could. I told her that we are very proud of her and regret that we would not be able to attend after all of this time. Since she writes about twice a week, it seems like we have been on campus with her the entire time. You remember that I told you in her last letter that she made all As. Well, we were not surprised because she always enjoyed reading, writing, and everything that you liked. She loved being like her big sister. So I am sure that she will be contacting you.

Since she is trying to cut down on expenses, she doesn't call very much. You know now that I think about it, we haven't had a call from her in about six months. Every time that she called, she had a cold and she didn't sound like herself, but she assured me that she was just fine. She also said that she never really knew us until she went away to college. Your father and I have really felt closer to her than we ever have. Ino, since you probably will be seeing her before I will, please tell her to call, charge it to my end, and that we can't wait to see her.

Oh, before I go, I heard from your Aunt Aimee the other day, and she asked about you. She wondered if you ever ask about her or if you ever talk about her visit a long time ago. I told her that you have never mentioned it, but that I would let you know that she asked about you. She is doing very well. Do you remember her last visit? You were about eleven. Well, it was so long ago, you probably don't.

Ino, since this will be Jamie's first Christmas with us in eight years, I am planning a family homecoming. I would like for you and Liam to come. It's been a long time since we have all been together.

Ino, just the other day I was thinking about the name that we gave you, and I think it fits you, don't you? Don't forget to tell Jamie to call and let me know what you decide.

Love,

Mother

I love the way that Mother always begins her letters with the season rather than the month. It's Mother! You are right, it is time for the family to get together this Christmas, and Liam would like that. Yes, Mother, I definitely feel that my name fits me perfectly, and you don't need to worry because your sister's secret is safe with me. What do you know, she did know. Well, I can't wait to read Jamie's letter.

While still pondering over what Mother said in her letter, I couldn't help but think about my Aunt Aimee again. Sometimes it seems like a lifetime ago, and at other times, it seems like it was only yesterday. Still, my sister is graduating; it's a special graduation, and that's what's important today. So I picked up my sister's letter and thought, *I hadn't heard from her in such a long time. I know that she is excited about graduation, but after reading Mother's letter, I am surprised that she didn't call to invite us. Since I am just hearing about it now, it's probably too late. I wonder if everything is all right.*

My sister's letter read,

October 19, 1994

Dear Sis,

How is life treating you? Hope that you are in good health. I wish that we could have kept in touch, but I was not allowed to communicate with anyone outside of these walls until now. Strange, isn't it? What I am about to tell you, you may find extremely hard to believe, but it's true. You know how I have always wanted to go away to school. Well, as you know I did about eight years ago, but what you don't know is what really happened. I haven't revealed this to anyone in our family, but I know that you will keep my secret until I decide what to do. Since Mom and Dad named you Ino, I know that telling you is like writing in a dairy, but with benefits. It has been an unforgettable experience, and I really need your help.

As you know, the family thinks that I am about to graduate from medical school, but what they don't know is that I have been under doctor's care for the last eight years. I didn't need the attention, but it was an unfortunate, unbelievable incident that was out of my control. This was a shock to me as I know that it will be for you. Please be patient while I try to explain.

I am sure that Mother told you how excited I was about the outstanding scholarship that I received to attend college in San Francisco. Well, on the very day that I arrived, everything changed. I called Mother to say that I had arrived safely and that I would contact them again very soon. I told her not to worry about me and I would write them the following week. Mother was delighted, and I felt that I was ready.

Since it was such a beautiful day and I had time to spare, I decided to leave my bags at the airport for a while and just take a stroll to see the city. With the weather being a sunny eighty-two degrees, the city was charged with excitement. So I walked out of the airport and across the street excited about my future. I thought about my four years at the university and then medical school. The thought that in eight years I would be a doctor played continuously in my mind and with an uncontrollable spirit. Even though I was just beginning, the end was quite vivid. So all I could think about was after all this time I had finally made it. I always wanted to live and study in a big city. This was a dream come true! The city was beautiful, and I thought that after I had seen enough for one day that I would get a taxi to take me back to the airport, but not now.

So I crossed one street after another up and down hills. It was truly amazing! There were more hills than I had ever seen before even in those movies that we used to watch about San Francisco. So I walked and walked, but as I was walking, I kept hearing a woman's voice saying, "Everyone, keep up. Stay together. Everyone walk this way." I thought that it was part of a tour group, and I would just walk with them for a while to see the city. We walked and walked and walked. Ino, I believe that we saw the entire city or at least it felt that way. Then something strange happened. I could see the sun setting in the distance. I looked at my watch and wondered where the time had gone. I realized that I had spent the entire day walking around the city and had done nothing else. So I started to stray away from the crowd and the girl that I had been talking to, but I was told that we must stay together. What were they talking about? I was from a small town, but this did not sound right.

So I approached the lady that had been speaking and said, "I am not part of this group. Where are we?" She did not say a word, just made a gesture to two men, and immediately we were all ushered onto a bus. Before I could do or say anything, we took off like a train. Ino, little did I know at the time where we were going or what was about to happen. It was particularly unnerving because no one spoke on the bus except for the driver and the lady that led the group. We visited many places that day, on and off the bus we went. I couldn't hear what they were saying, and I had never seen any of those people before, yet they seemed to know me. Everyone seemed content, but we were not allowed to speak. At least when I did I was told that everything would be okay because we would be back at The Home in a few minutes. I didn't like the sound of that, so I said, "I will just be getting off at the next stop." Everyone looked at me like I had spoken a foreign language, and the journey continued. I thought it was because of the silence rule. Still, I protested, but it was useless. The lady that had told us to stay together just walked up to me, touched me on the shoulder, and said, "It's okay, Jamie, everything is okay." I gave her *the look*. You remember *the look*. So I sat there wondering, *how does she know my name? How? What is going on? Where is The Home? How can I get off this bus? What will happen when I don't show up at the university? They will be expecting me. Oh nooo! Since I called Mother when I arrived, they would not have any reason to worry for a while. What had I done?*

At that moment, Ino, I had a strange feeling like this had happened before, but when? Have you ever had an empty feeling or a feeling of what's next? That's the way that I felt that day, but I had to shake it off.

In the meantime, the bus pulled into The Home, and we were all given a cup of water, a sugar cube, and were taken to our rooms. I did not drink the water nor did I eat the cube, but I pretended and acted like the others. They walked around like they were in a trance, but they seemed happy and no one harmed them. I was told that I would still be in the room with a lady named Annie, but I didn't know Annie. The lady from the bus said she had been my roommate the previous year. Well, I knew that something was really wrong because that was my first day in San Francisco, but how did she know my name? Had there been another person that looked like me with the same name? Was this possible? Yes, it was, and this is what I discovered. Brace yourself.

There had been a patient at The Home named Jamie just like me. She had been brought here by her family for the purpose of rest, relaxation, and to get her composure. She had been a student at the university and had worked tirelessly in the field of medicine and needed time to get herself together. Therefore, every time I mentioned the university, they thought that I was her, Jamie A. Moore, but I was Jamie E. Moore. After many years of insisting that I shouldn't be here and that this was a mistake, they finally read an article in *The Montavian*, the local newspaper, about a Jamie Moore that had pushed an older lady out of the way of an oncoming car near the university and had saved her life.

The headlines read, *"Local University Medical Student, Jamie A. Moore, Saves the Life of a Longtime Resident."* The red flag went up, and the lady in charge called me in. After all this time, they listened to me, took tests, and realized that I was not their Jamie Moore. The day of their outing eight years ago was the day that I had arrived in town, and when Jamie saw the uncanny resemblance, it was her opportunity to stray away from the crowd. She was the girl that I had been talking to, but I didn't notice her as much as she had noticed me. Then when I looked away, she became a part of the crowd, and I became a part of the group. This is what they surmised. She walked away that day with my identity, and I unknowingly took her place. I had lost eight years of my life. What were they supposed to do? Basically, there was little that they could do. So I was released with an apology and a small sum of money to compensate for the last eight years of my life. Ino, my mouth dropped wide-open.

I couldn't help but be angry and disappointed, eight looong years. Was this time wasted? What did I learn from this? I know that everything happens for a reason, but I couldn't understand the reason for this. What would happen to Jamie A. Moore? She had proven to her family that she was all right, had completed college, medical school, and saved a life. Wow! What had this done for me or to me? Where was my family all of this time? Had they looked for me? Were we close as a family, or had they sent me off to college and had forgotten about me? Ino, today is the day that I was supposed to graduate from medical school, but today is the day that I am leaving The Home. What does this mean? Ironic, isn't it? Was this a graduation from or to? What was the lesson learned? *I DO NOT KNOW!* Was the lesson for me, Jamie E. Moore and my family, or Jamie A. Moore and her family, or all of us? Should I eventually tell our parents? All of these questions were left unanswered.

Ino, I told you when I began this letter that you would find this hard to believe, but I know that you were not prepared for this. I was given my purse, an allotment for my trouble, and an apology. Before I leave San Francisco, I am going back to that locker to see if anything remained at the airport. After all this time, I don't expect to find anything, but I am going anyway. I still can't believe this. Ino, I remember your address and about the time that you receive this letter, I should be arriving at your home, and we will have a long talk about what you know and where I should go from here. Strange, isn't it? This is the day that I should be receiving my degree and a new life, but it's the day that I have been given my freedom and a new chance at life. See you soon. What am I to do?

Your loving sis,

Jamie

This can't be real! This just can't be real! My poor sister has had an unfortunate experience. Then I thought about Jamie's question and what a question it was. Yes, Jamie, I have had that empty feeling and that feeling of what's next. It was that night that Aunt Aimee arrived. You were only seven, but you had it too. What do you know?

Jamie will be arriving soon, and won't she be surprised when she reads Mother's letter. I can't wait to see her!

Chapter 5

Revelation II

The golden sun played peekaboo through the trees as another day was coming to an end. The stillness and peacefulness of the day and the informative revelations had left me expectant, yet silently yearning for closure on all fronts. While still in disbelief and reading Jamie's letter for the third time, I heard a car door slam. I lowered the letter only to see my sister paying the taxi driver and retrieving her luggage. Crying tears of joy, I sprang to my feet, rushed down the steps, and grabbed my sister like an eagle protecting her young.

"I missed you, little sis. Are you all right?" I said and noticed that she appeared rested as well as puzzled.

"I'm okay, and I really missed you, Ino. This was an unbelieeevable situation," she uttered as her voice trembled a bit.

"Jamie, it's hard to comprehend this!"

"It is for me too, Ino. I just can't understand why and why me." Jamie said a bit more composed now.

"You know, Ino, if Jamie hadn't saved that lady from that oncoming car, I could still be at the Home," Jamie said with a look that indicated that that thought just came to her.

"Jamie, let's try not to think about that. Everything worked out the way that it was supposed to, and you're here."

Jamie walked slower now with her luggage in her hand as though she was thinking about a what-if saga.

Soon she said as though she was looking for assurance, "Things will get better. Right, Ino?"

"Right, Jamie," I added with certainty.

The words kept coming and so did the tears until I said, "Come in and let's get you settled. We'll talk some more, and I'll let you read Mother's letter."

For a brief period, the only sounds that could be heard were the creaking of the door, the chirping of the crickets high in the trees in the distance, and the geese seemingly very close by.

As we entered the house, Jamie uttered through the sounds of the crickets, "Itttt's good to be here, Ino. It's really good. I have missed my family, and I can't wait to read Mother's letter."

I thought that I would make small talk to lighten the load that we were carrying at the time, even though Jamie looked a bit more relaxed now. So I said, "I just received your letter today and here you are. You estimated that just right."

"I guess that I did," she said.

"Jamie, I know that this has been a very difficult time for you, and that you have gone through a lot, but you do realize that everything is going to be all right."

"I do."

"You must believe that," I said as I gave her a bear hug. At that moment, I reflected briefly when my mom and I had our little secret.

"I do, sis. I really do. I just can't understand why."

"You know, Jamie, a lot of things happen that we just don't understand, but with faith, time and patience, we'll get through them."

"I know, but right now it's just so hard," Jamie said while shaking her head.

"Have a seat, Jamie, and we'll try to sort it out. Would you like a cold glass of lemonade, a glass of ice tea, or some hot chocolate?"

"At this moment, I think that I'll have a tall glass of ice water."

"Are you hungry? I have had such an unexpected and unbelievable day that I have not cooked anything."

"No, I had a slice of sausage pizza, a toss salad, and a Coke when I went to the airport, but thank you."

"Just water then."

"Just water."

"Coming up."

I poured a tall glass of ice water, and as I turned to hand her the glass, I saw tears falling from the corners of her eyes like a waterfall, but she grabbed a handkerchief from her jacket pocket and quickly wiped them away. Since she didn't want me to see them, I pretended that I didn't and only said, "Are you sure that you are all right?"

She nodded, and with that, I replied, "Now I won't say begin at the beginning because after reading your letter over and over again, I know what happened and how it happened, but like you said, why is the question. The more that I think about it, I believe that the other Jamie is the only one that can answer that question."

"Ino, I believe that you are right, but it may be hard to get in touch with her. She knew the day that she took over my identity that there would be repercussions. So there's a possibility that she may not want to talk to me."

"I don't think that it's going to be as hard as you think."

"Why do you say that, Ino?"

"I believe that you need to read the letter that I received from Mother earlier today. You see, I received both of your letters today. Coincidence?"

"Destiny. How is Mother? What did she say? Has the family been looking for me? Ino, were you concerned about me?"

You could hear the longing for family and also the why echoing through her words. She hadn't said anything about that earlier, but she did have a lot on her mind, I thought.

"Jamie, I believe that once you read Mother's letter, most of your questions will be answered, and then we'll talk. But don't be surprised at what you might discover."

"What do you mean?"

"Here's the letter. Just read it first, and then we'll talk."

"I'll try, but I don't know if I can promise you that."

I watched my sister unfold the letter, take a sniff, and then smile. This was a confirmation that the lavender scent was our Mother's fragrance. I had never noticed it before, but she did. My sister noticed everything. Then she slipped off her chestnut brown loafers, curled upon the couch, and began reading. She looked like she was at home, and that made me feel good after everything that she had been through.

She no longer had those thick long black ponytails that added extra time to the morning routine. She had grown up, and we had missed it. She didn't go to college as soon as she graduated from high school because of our other sisters and brothers. So she took a job for a while at the same Fireside Nursing Home where I had worked after graduation and saved her money, applied for scholarships until one day she received one. It hasn't been easy for any of us, but we never gave up. Mother always told us that there is a season for everything, and I know that this is Jamie's season for total fulfillment.

Watching her now reminded me when she was in junior high school curled upon the couch reading the novels assigned for Mrs. Hudson's class. She always had a book to read. As I watched her facial expression and her eyes widen then lower and her mouth drop in shock, I knew what she was thinking. She was probably thinking the very same thing that I was thinking or more since she was directly affected.

With sadness and disbelief in her eyes, Jamie cried, "This girl not only took my place at the university, but with my family also! How could she, Ino? How could she?"

"I don't know. This I cannot explain, but can you understand why I never called you or tried to look for you? We, the family and I, never knew anything was wrong. I only discovered it when I received your letter and I had to read it three times, but the family doesn't know."

"So she wrote to Mother at least two times a week, and Mother kept you informed. What about holidays? Didn't you find it strange that I never came home for breaks or at the end of each school year?"

"I did at first, but you, she, wrote Mother that you, she, wanted to save on expenses and that at other times you, she, went home with some of your friends that lived close by."

"What about at Christmastime? Ino, that's my favorite time of the year. You know that I wouldn't have missed Christmas with my family."

"I felt that, Jamie, but you had your reasons. There was one Christmas that I remember you, she, spent it with one of your, her, closest friends because her family invited you, her, to go out of the country. Mother said that you were so excited, so she wrote you that it was fine, but the family would miss you. Everything that we did was out of love for you. We never thought anything about it because you, she, wrote all the time and seemed to be very happy. We felt that you were growing up, and as much as we missed you, we did not want to keep you from being happy and enjoying college life. Can you somewhat understand that?"

"I can, but for eight years. What was—"

"Jamie, try to remember that we had no reason to believe otherwise."

"You are right," Jamie said somewhat calmer now.

"You noticed in Mother's letter she said that they never felt closer to you than they do now, and you, she, said the same thing. You, she, said it was like you were seeing them for the first time or getting to know them all over again."

"Well, I guess it was for her since she really didn't know them."

"I know that this may be hard for you to comprehend, little sis, but it is for me also."

"Ino, this is getting harder and harder to believe. If I wasn't actually involved, I wouldn't believe this. We must get in touch with Jamie A. Moore."

"Like I told you before, I don't think it will be that hard."

"After reading Mother's letter, I believe that you are right."

"Jamie, it's been a long day. Let's get some rest, and in the morning, we will decide what to do. This has gone on long enough. We need to find out why and decide whether to tell the family or not."

"You are right. Thank you, sis."

"For what, Jamie?"

"Thank you for being my sister and for just being you. I just didn't know what to do, but I thought coming here would help me. I just want you to know that as soon as I arrived, a peaceful feeling came over me. I don't know what it was. It was like you are with family now, just relax. Even though I was confused, and I am sure that you sensed it, I knew that everything was going to be all right. Do you understand what I mean?"

"I do. I usually have that feeling every time I go down to visit Mother and the rest of the family. Sometimes I think about moving back, but I just love living here."

"There's a feeling of peace. Maybe it's just being with family again."

"Maybe it is, but let's not get started again, we need to get some rest. Are you sure that you don't want a snack or a cup of hot chocolate before turning in?"

"I'm sure."

"Okay, but I think I'll make me a cup with extra marshmallows. We'll begin again in the morning. You can take this bedroom, and I will be sleeping in the bedroom two doors down on the left. I hope that you will be comfortable, and don't worry because everything is going to be all right. Do you need anything?"

"No, not a thing."

"Don't be discouraged, Jamie. Things will change."

"I know they will, Ino. I am just ready now!"

"I know, but after eight years you have proven that you can handle this."

"You're right, again."

"Are you okay?"

"I am."

"See you in the morning then," I said as I walked toward the kitchen."

"Good night, Ino," Jamie said with a sigh of relief.

Chapter 6

A Lesson Learned

After many eventful and unexpected revelations the previous day and a peaceful night's sleep, I was looking forward to the day ahead and the discoveries to come. Ironically at that moment, recollections of the past seemed to creep into my mind as I was preparing breakfast. The kitchen was cozy and had that warm and comfortable feeling that you get on Thanksgiving morning, a sense of family. The colors of fall and the anticipation of the holiday season were at hand. The smell of the bacon, the homemade buttermilk biscuits, apple butter, scrambled eggs, and grits reminded me of our mother's kitchen when we were younger. I prepared it for my sister because right now she needed to be reminded about the love of her family. Even though my sister's visit had just begun, it was the kind of visit that you wanted to continue for a while. I hadn't seen Jamie in eight years, and it was just nice to have her here. Since I moved to Kentucky many years ago, this was something that I had missed. Even though, at times, it reminds me of my hometown, it still gives me a warm feeling to have my family around. So my sister and I sat across the kitchen table and feasted in silence until she said, "This is just what I needed, Ino. Sometimes you remind me of Mom, and that's good, real good. Thank you."

"No thanks needed. Since Liam travels a lot for his company, I don't cook as much as I used to. It's nice to have someone to cook for, so just eat up," I said with a lump in my throat, thinking about the meals that I used to prepare for Liam before his business life became his life.

"I was so involved in my own situation, I didn't even ask about my brother-in-law. How is he?"

"He is doing fine. It just seems like he's always working."

"Tell him that next time that I am in town, that it would be nice to see him again. It has been so long."

"I will tell him."

"Sis, I need to read you something. I think that it could change everything."

Instead of looking at me, it appeared that she was looking through me. Her demeanor had changed, and she was about business. Then I noticed that she had brought her purse to the table, but I didn't question it. Knowing my sister, I knew that she had her reasons.

"I told you yesterday that this situation was unbelievable, and I just made another discovery," Jamie added.

"What was it? When?"

"It happened this morning. Well, last night and this morning."

"Really? I thought that I heard you moving around when I came past your bedroom, but I didn't want to disturb you. So what has happened?"

"It was something that we didn't expect, Ino."

"Like what? Well, I'm sure that after everything that you have been through, you can deal with whatever it is."

"Don't be so sure. Brace yourself again. During the early morning hours, something caused me to wake up, and I couldn't get back to sleep for a while. I tossed and turned, sat up in the bed, then lay back down again just staring at the ceiling."

"What was it?" I asked immediately.

"I don't know. Since I couldn't get back to sleep for a while, I lay there in silence, and in a low whisper, I heard one word and I didn't know why until this morning," Jamie said with a sense of peace resonating from her voice.

Well, this only aroused my curiosity more, and I said, "And what was that word?"

She looked at me calmly and said, "Forgive."

"You only heard one word."

"Yes, and I felt extremely calm, and I immediately turned over and went back to sleep. Like I said, I didn't understand it until this morning."

"Details, Jamie, details!"

"Well, I got up this morning and couldn't help but be reminded of the feeling that I had during the night, and that word just played over and over in my mind. Still, I couldn't put it together until I was looking through this purse that was given back to me before I left The Home. I noticed this white envelope protruding from the back pocket. I usually notice everything, but this wasn't noticeable. I pulled it out, opened it, and you wouldn't believe what it said."

"What? What?"

"Let me just read it to you."

October 19

Jamie, let me begin by saying, please forgive me. My name is Jamie A. Moore, but I'm sure that you realized that just from the first line. I am sure that you did not expect to hear from me, but I had to try today. I know what I did was wrong, but when you told me about your family, I knew that I was missing something. I really acted without thinking. I am sorry! Even though this situation was difficult, you cannot imagine what your family has given me. My parents have always traveled and never really made time for me. I know that you are thinking that that is not an excuse for what I have done, but please believe me this was not planned. The day that it happened, everything just seemed to fall into place. I saw you, we talked, you shared, we attended the same university, had the same name. Well, I am sure that you know everything by now.

Jamie, since the newspaper article, things have changed for me and my family. They know now, and I know that things have changed for you and yours. I have not contacted your mother since the last letter inviting her to my graduation. I really didn't think that they would attend, but at that point I wanted to meet them. They seemed to be so caring and nonjudgmental. I realize that this situation should have ended before now, but how could I. I started to believe it myself. For the very first time in my life there were people that were interested in me and the things that concerned me. You cannot imagine having a loving family like yours because you have always had them! This is something that I never had but desperately wanted. I know that my parents love me, but they just didn't know how to show it. I needed them, but they didn't realize that placing me in The Home wasn't the answer. They do now! So my parents and I would like to talk with you about this situation. Jamie, I know that it may be hard for you to see it from my point of view, but I hope that you will at least try. My parents said that you and your family have brought out the good in us. My parents and I have never been able to share, show love, make plans about our future, talk about the holidays and really look forward to them together. We have never done this, but we are now! Jamie, this is because of you and your family. Please don't take your family for granted. I guess you are saying, look who is giving advice, but you have what most people are seeking. My parents said they have learned a lot from your family but told me to make an effort to set this right. I know that eight years is a long time, but we would like to make it up to you. Since I stole something from you and I was robbed of my childhood, my parents would like to pay for you to go to college and medical school, if it's not too late.

Jamie, I came to The Home on your last day there, but I couldn't face you. So I wrote this letter, asked the lady at the desk to give it to you, and left. I am not a selfish person. I was just a very lonely person, and I was helped by your family. This was hard to write, but I hope that you will understand. You saved me, and I hope that I helped you too (in some way). If you are interested in talking, my number is written on the other side or we can just go our separate ways. I hope that you will decide the former rather than the latter. I also hope that you can find it in your heart to forgive me, and let me try to set things right.

Regretfully,

Jamie A. Moore

"Well, Ino, what do you think? Was it as hard for you as it was for me?"

"It was. You know, little sis, I wanted to interrupt you several times while you were reading, but I just couldn't. That was about as unexpected as anything that I have ever heard, but sincere."

"Very sincere," Jamie repeated.

"Wow! A curveball! You have been thrown a curveball!"

"That's exactly what this is! Exactly. You know, Ino, when I first read this letter, I was surprised at my response."

"What do you mean?"

"Well, I was surprised because just yesterday I knew very little about Jamie A., only what she did, but today, I know her and everything about her, and that makes a difference. Do you understand about not really knowing someone until something happens?" Jamie said questioning, but with an air of realization.

"Yes, I do, Jamie. I have gone through that before. Then you realize that everyone has problems, and that we are not different, that we can help one another if we choose to, and if we chose to we can't lose."

"Right."

"Jamie, there is also a peaceful feeling that you get when the battle has been won that lets us know that you are doing the right thing. Sometimes it takes longer than others, but you'll know. You have prayed over this, right?"

"I have, and right now that is exactly what I am experiencing. So you really do understand, Ino?"

"I do, little sis."

"Ino, what can you say after that?"

"Nothing, absolutely nothing. You helped her, now she is helping you to see the difference it's making in all of our lives. Oh my goodness, Jamie, even though the ball is in your court, you must remember what you told me."

"I know, so now do you understand what the word meant?" Jamie said with assurance that the answer was apparent.

"I do. In other words, you were given the answer last night before the question was asked."

"You are correct. It wasn't what I expected to find out, but all of my questions have been answered."

"They have. Sometimes it comes when you least expect it, but usually when you are ready to accept it. Do you understand?"

"I do now, but it hit me hard especially when she said that I helped her. At that moment, I was thinking this helped you, but not me. Still, the more that I thought about it, Ino, she was right. I didn't get the education that I wanted, but it definitely was a lesson learned. Through this situation, I learned a lot about myself, my family, and others, but most of all I learned about forgiveness, love, unselfishness, peace, faith, life, and I'm still learning. I'm sorry, Ino, I didn't mean to preach to you, but it's just amazing."

"It is, Jamie."

"Yes, I did go through something, but like our parents have always said sometimes you have to go through something to get to something. Now I understand that. Maybe God was trying to show me that that was Jamie A. Moore's path, and through my experience I too found my path."

"Sometimes we are just too busy to listen, and we miss out on so much, Jamie."

"Ino, I never felt as fulfilled as I did on the days when they were shorthanded that I worked with the people at The Home listening to their problems, coaching them and helping them. I think at the time I was overly concerned about my situation and couldn't see it from any other standpoint, but now that I think about it, it felt really good to help others in that way. You know, Ino, everything happens for a reason, and I now know what I want to do with my life. After eight long years, I finally know where I am going and what I want to do with my life. Eerie, isn't it? What seemed to be the worst thing that could have happened to me turned out to be the best thing that could have happened to me."

"I know, little sis, and since like you said the answer was given before the question was asked, then you know what to do, right?"

"Right, Ino, but I had to find out for myself."

"Jamie, it happened to me a long time ago, not in that way, but with the same results. You must believe that everything works out for your good."

"This was a hard lesson, but a lesson learned. I will contact Jamie tomorrow and tell her that she wasn't the only one that received an education, and yes, I will forgive her. I may even take her up on going back to school, but in psychology because I have many years of experience under my belt." Jamie said with a hearty laugh.

"Tomorrow also we'll call Mother and tell her that we are going to pay her and the family a visit and that we have something to tell them, but today I am going to take you out to lunch and celebrate your new career and your new life. Still—"

"Ino, that sounds like a winner, but what is it?"

"Are you sure that you don't want to call Jamie first?"

"You're right, as always. This is something that just can't wait, and there are a few unresolved issues."

"A few! Plus, you never know what else you might discover!"

"More discoveries, you think there could be more?"

"You had one curveball!"

"True, but I hope that's all."

I watched my sister as she pulled the letter out of her purse again and just stared at the paper for a moment.

"Ino, everything is happening so fast! I didn't expect this!"

"That's usually the way that it happens."

"Would you mind staying close by?"

"I wouldn't mind at all, Jamie, but since you have prayed, it's going to be all right."

While I watched my sister dial the number, I knew that she really needed to do this. Then I noticed that she had settled comfortably on the couch, appeared at ease, and was ready for the outcome. As the smell of the lavender vanilla-scented candle that I had lit earlier permeated throughout the room, I breathed a sigh of relief as I experienced a sense of peace. I slowly walked into the kitchen, sat at the breakfast bar, took out my pad and pen, and waited for-

"Hello, hello, may I speak to Jamie? Jamie, this is Jamie E. Moore. I can understand that you didn't think that I would call, but I knew that closure was necessary. Well, I didn't expect to find out what I did in your letter. You are correct. I was angry, disappointed, and I did go through every emotion, but I need to tell you something. No, I didn't call to chastise you, just to say that I have forgiven you. Yes, I am serious!"

As I looked up from my writing pad, I noticed that my sister was all right because she was walking around and around the coffee

table and talking, but with a glow that looked like the morning sun. She was at peace, and she was making sure that Jamie A. felt it also. Every few moments I looked up from what I was doing and noticed that everything was under control. After about an hour, I heard my sister say, "Yes, I will be contacting you, very soon." *This I did not expect!* I thought.

As she put down the phone, she appeared in front of me in the kitchen quicker than I could bat my eyes.

"Ino, did you hear? Did you hear?" she said extremely excited.

"I did, but I only heard what you said, so fill in the details."

"We talked like it was something that was supposed to happen."

"Maybe, it was."

"Jamie A. wants me to contact her after I talk with Mom and Dad. She said that she has come to know my parents and would like to keep in touch, if they are willing. That their advice to her while she was going through this situation has been a blessing, and that even though at the time her motives were selfish, she isn't."

"What else did she say?"

"She stated again how sorry she was, and that they meant it about paying for my education. There is more!" My sister blurted out with a loud roar.

"What more could there be?"

"She said that her family has never communicated the way that they are doing now. That she has missed so much with her family and while discovering her new career, she realized what they were missing. Are you ready, Ino?"

"For what?"

"Remember that you said don't be surprised at what I might discover."

"Yes."

"Here it is! Jamie said that her family has decided to open a home for people that are having problems like she was having, but with counseling sessions, assistance programs, jobs for the people afterward, and much more. She indicated that they have not worked out all the details yet, but since they took something from me, they would like for me and my family to be a part of it."

"Are you kidding?"

"No! They would like for Mom and Dad to consider joining with them to help others the way they helped her. I told her that I would be going home and that I would present this to them, and we would get back with them. Ino, there's that curveball. Once again, I did not expect this!"

"Jamie, neither did I, but how do you feel about this?"

"I'm okay with it."

"So am I."

At that moment I just knew because I had the same feeling that I had experienced many years ago the day that my Aunt Aimee left, and I knew that everything was the way that it was supposed to be. I just knew. Then I looked at Jamie, and she smiled as she was about to go get ready for lunch, and I knew by the sparkle in her eyes, the pep in her step, and the song that she hummed as she passed me in the hall that she felt it too. My sister was all right. Through times past, we have learned and continue to learn that with faith, time, and patience, things will turn out for our good.

Chapter 7

Who Really Knows?

As I sat in the kitchen at the breakfast bar writing and waiting for Jamie to get dressed, the events of the day were quite vivid. It had been a truly remarkable day, and it wasn't over yet. While sitting there I began to think about Liam and the message on the answering machine that he would be home mid-November, and I was looking forward to it. That would be a good time to tell him about Mother's plan to get all of us together for Christmas. Jamie was so concerned about the information about Jamie A. that she didn't say anything about the Christmas homecoming. I will talk to her about that during lunch today.

"I'm ready, now! Do you think this fuchsia top match with these smoky gray jeans?"

"I like it. Jamie, when I started this experience I thought that I had all the answers to what I wanted in my life. I thought that I wanted to be an artist, and for years that's what I've done."

"Right, but what are you saying?" Jamie asked with deep concern.

"I am saying that all of these years I have felt a disconnection with my work, and I did not realize why until you were going through your situation. Liam tried to tell me many times, so did my closet friends, and Mother, but I wasn't listening. After all this time, I believe that God was trying to tell me something."

"Do you? What were they trying to tell you?"

"They were trying to tell me to do what I have always had a passion for."

"What's that? Ino, I remember, writing."

"Right, writing. I have always loved to write. Maybe that's the reason that Liam's job takes him away so much. It gives me the time I need to write. I can't wait to tell Liam. So through your experience, I found what I have always wanted to do. I have been doing it for a long time when I was not painting, but who would have thought that when I was helping others I would also find my joy."

"That's true, sis. It happened for me," Jamie added.

"I know, just when you think it's over, it isn't."

"Wow! Ino."

"Jamie, you just don't know how I got here. Before we go to lunch, I need to tell you something."

Jamie sat down immediately on the couch and positioned herself to receive what I was about to impart. My little sister had grown up, and she wanted to help.

"You listened to me, sis, so just take your time. Now you are giving me practice for my new profession."

"I know. You know, little sis, it doesn't matter how old you are, how much money you have, how many degrees you get, whether you are the president of a company or the employee, a lawyer, a caregiver, a teacher, or a student everyone has something to give. Also, we can all learn from whatever we go through—successes, failures, or life's lesson. Jamie, I have learned so much, and in the middle or maybe at the end you find out what God was trying to show you all along. Sometimes we miss it, fail the test, and have to take it over, but there is always another chance. He never gives up on us, and we should never give up on ourselves or on others."

"You know what, Ino, we thought that we had it all worked out, didn't we? Then just about the time we were about to go to lunch, you were given the bottom line. How did you know?"

"Jamie, there's an uneasiness that you have until everything is the way that it's supposed to be. Just like Mother and Daddy always say after you have been tested, when you feel that inner peace, then you just know that you know that you know."

"And you know," Jamie added.

"Didn't you, Jamie?"

"I did."

"And I do. Let's go to lunch, Jamie."

"Thanks, sis."

"No, not me. *Thank God.*"

"You're right, *thank God.*"

The sequel to *The Peace Within* entitled *A Christmas Homecoming* will be available in December 2010. It is the story of the Moore family after eight years apart. It is truly a celebration! Get to know them all over again and have a heartfelt Merry Christmas like you have never experienced before. Experience the blessings of this remarkable family and share their joy as you remember yours. Thank you for everything and have a blessed day. *Reserve your copy today!*